# Gabi Wolf
# Wonder Worlds
## Volume 2
### Coloring Book

Copyright © 2023 Gabi Wolf, Berlin
All rights reserved.

All illustrations published in this book are protected by copyright and may only be used commercially with the express written permission of the author. Reproduction or distribution of the contents of the book is prohibited and will be prosecuted under civil and criminal law. This applies in particular to reproductions, translations, microfilms, and storage and distribution in electronic systems. The author disclaims any liability for damages of any kind or misuse of this book.

1. Publication in 2023
ISBN: 979-8399311005
Independently published
Cover & Illustrations: Gabi Wolf

# Welcome to the Wonderworlds

Our earth is full of wonders. Many of them are only seen at a second glance, and some only exist in our imagination. When I walk through nature, I often imagine this fantasy world exists, and suddenly I see busy elves and dwarves going about their daily chores everywhere. They lead a happy life in tiny houses on flowering meadows. Wouldn't it be great if these wonder worlds really existed?

Take a journey through these wonder worlds while colouring. Add your own ideas and bring them to life with bright colours. With this way you can create your own little wonder world.

## www.gabiwolf.de

## ⓘ ⓕ  gabisgrafiken

# Tips forthe coloring

Crayons are best suited for coloring. They offer a wide variety of options by blending or applying in several layers. So you can achieve many wonderful effects.

If you want to use felt pens or watercolors, check them out first on the color test pages at the end of the book. This will tell you if too much of the paint has been applied and is visible through the paper. Don't paint over the same spot too many times in a row.

Place a sheet or two of paper under the image you are working on. This is a good underlay and prevents indentation or transfer of color to the page below.

The pages are printed on one side. So you can cut out pictures that you particularly like and hang them up.

## I wish you a lot of fun coloring!

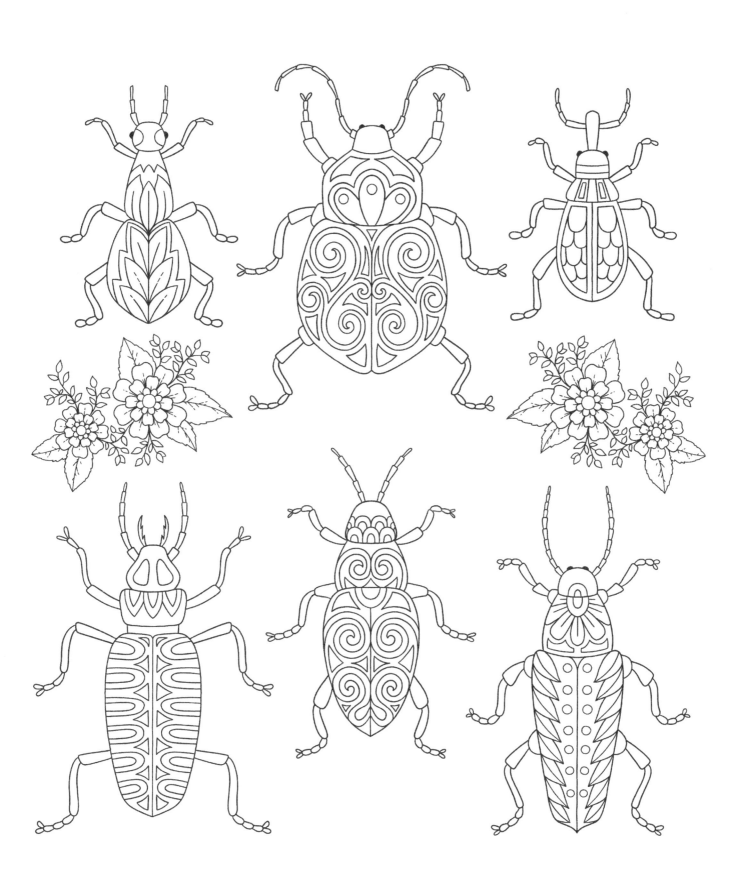

# Color Test Page

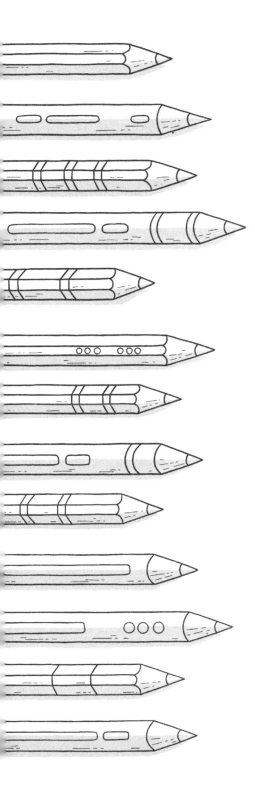

# Color Test Page

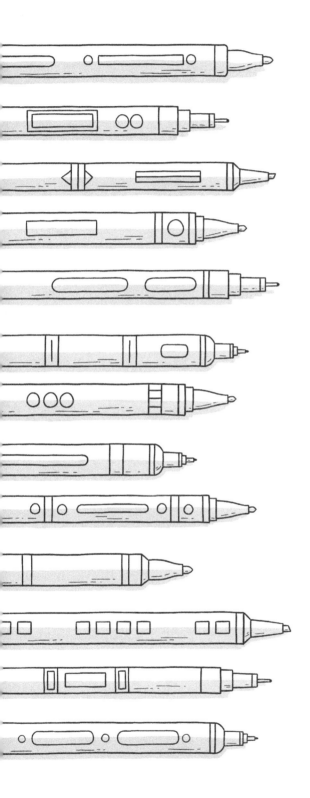

# Color Test Page

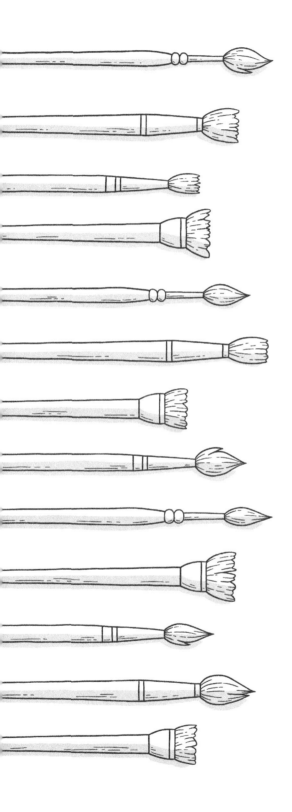

Foto: www.lichthelden-berlin.de

Thank you so much for choosing this coloring book!
I hope you enjoyed coloring it.

For more information about my coloring books and
illustrations, visit my website or social media.

## www.gabiwolf.de

 gabisgrafiken

# More Coloring Books from Gabi Wolf

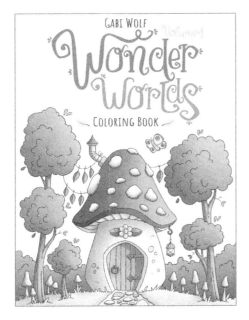

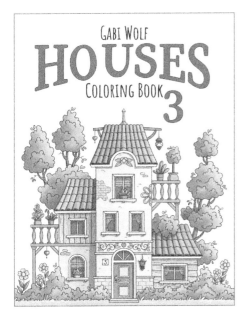
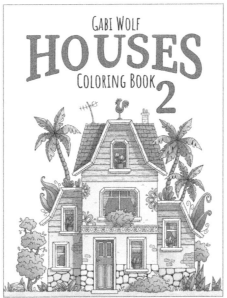
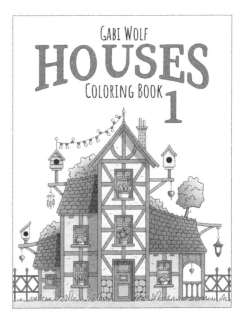
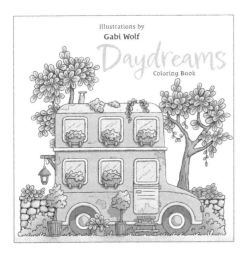

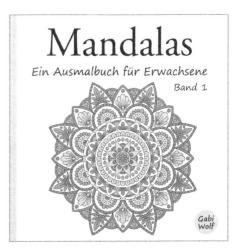

Copyright © 2023 Gabi Wolf, Berlin
Cover & Illustrationen: Gabi Wolf
All rights reserved
Theodor-Brugsch-Str. 2, 13125 Berlin
Germany

Made in the USA
Middletown, DE
08 August 2025

11938571R00044